A COURSE IN CONFIDENCE

A COURSE IN CONFIDENCE

Align. Evolve. Ascend

SARESA MARIE COOPER

Kae-oh Publishing

Contents

Dedication — vi

1. The Tan Suit — 1
2. The Mont — 5
3. The Love — 7
4. The Mustard Lexus — 10
5. The "Friends" — 13
6. The "Money" & The "Thief" — 15
7. The Gut — 18
8. Saresa's Prayer — 21
9. The Pandemic — 23
10. The Lady Who Harvest — 25

To Sarah, Naomi, and Yvonne

I cried many tears writing this. Through my pain it is my prayer you enjoy it!

To the three most important ladies of my life and lifetime. What you have contributed to me words, labels, or expressions couldn't begin to comprehend. You supported me before you knew I existed, you lifted me before I even took a loss, you loved me before I could define what love was. Your blood purified me like the ocean washing over rocks. Your smile penetrated me like the sand under my feet at the ocean's edge. You, you, and you laid the foundations for my healing. I wouldn't have this opportunity had you not given up so many. I couldn't laugh so friendly had I not experienced your pain. Through you, I inherit all that I am!

Copyright © 2022 by Saresa Marie Cooper

All rights reserved. No part of this publication may be reproduced, stored or transmitted in any form or by any means, electronic, mechanical, photocopying, recording, scanning, or otherwise without written permission from the publisher. It is illegal to copy this book, post it to a website, or distribute it by any other means without permission.
Saresa Marie Cooper asserts the moral right to be identified as the author of this work.

ISBN: 978-1-7372797-4-7

Published by Kae-oh Publishing

First Printing, 2022

I

The Tan Suit

Confidence is key, confidence is key, confidence is key... I remember hearing that phrase at various points in my life but never truly understanding just how true it would be for me and others who surrounded me.

"You didn't turn in your resume?"

"Nope, I sure didn't."

"Well girl you better go in there with the confidence of the world!"

I had on my tan, tall-leg split suit that tied in the front with a dark brown belt with the tall-leg mahogany brown boot to match with the perfect three and a half inch heel. Your girl was flying and I was only fifteen, maybe sixteen years old. Oh, and my hair—I forgot to tell you about that! I had the nice laid bob weave with the highlights swooped to the side, with a hint of makeup and a touch of lip gloss. I mean, I was doing the damn thing! But the fact still remained I was unprepared.

So then the next question that naturally arose was whether I was going to let my being ill-prepared stifle me or strengthen my position. I chose the latter and it worked wonderfully in my favor.

This was my first serious competition I entered. For my family, being in BPA (short for Business Professionals of America) was a big deal. My elder brother did it before me and his first year in competition he didn't fare as well as I did. It was my responsibility to do better!

The next day, after going into the job interview competition, we patiently waited for the results. Finally, they were announcing the winners. . . . This was my opportunity and my brother was in my ear the whole time.

"Third place, Sheila McKenzie."

"Oh she always wins. Wait, I wonder who outdid her this year!"

"Second place, almost first place except she didn't turn in her resume, Saresa Cooper."

I don't think I've ever seen my brother so excited since or after.

"You actually beat Sheila!"

I walked slowly and confidently, claiming the reward I knew I greatly deserved because of the energy I invested in that venture.

Although this is one of my earliest memories of my audacious confidence working in my favor, I have many stories of my humility and timidity working against me.

* * *

"Do you think you're pretty?"

At that moment I am not sure I knew how to answer that question or even what question was truly being asked of me. My first thought was "doesn't everyone think they are pretty?" But instead I answered my idiot classmate in such a disrespectful manner to myself.

"I guess, or I think, or honestly I don't know. Why do you ask?"

"I ask because I really want to know what you think because I don't see it, I just wondered if you did?"

I think back to that moment and realize how I stepped out of my power. I had the nerve to feel ugly in that moment because someone else deemed it necessary to tell me I was. I now know that anyone determined to make me or anyone feel *less than* is in deep pain and doesn't deserve acknowledgment to any degree with the hatred they wish to project onto others.

We must always remember, it is not flesh and blood that we wrestle but principalities (Eph. 6:12). As I matured into my confidence, I realized this important fact and was able to garner my confidence much easier when I kept it in mind!

I can remember thinking I was unattractive as a young lady because I was dark skinned, had a large gap in my teeth, I was always the tallest in the class and always the largest! And honey, listen, when I was in elementary school it was worse. I had all those traits plus I was half blind with a patch over my left eye with red, large-rimmed glasses. I was called a pirate every day I went to school with that patch over my eye. I hated it, and I hated my mom and my ophthalmologist for making me wear it!

I am, however, grateful for those experiences. They have paved the foundation for the astronomical confidence I have in my life at thirty-five years old. I gained this confidence through many trials and triumphs that without I would not be the fine young lady I have turned out to be today!

2

The Mont

It was 2013 and it was, so far, the worst time of my life. I was twenty-six and recently unemployed after getting fired from what I thought would be my chosen career path in law after obtaining my paralegal degree. It so happened, life would take me in another direction that was much more fitting for me.

A friend of mine at the time wanted to go out to celebrate her success and, being the friend I was, I went. Little did I know I would meet the man of my dreams which turned quickly into a nightmare seven months later! I moved in with him after knowing him for all of twenty-four hours—yes, twenty-four hours, I said that right! I was in such a low place, love was all I wanted and I would do anything I felt necessary to feel it or obtain a semblance of it!

Well, he did warn me that if I ever cheated he would hit me. I did speak to someone else and he hit me so hard that this five foot nine inch woman weighing about two hundred and sixty pounds at the time flew off the bed and hit the closet door. The pain was so destabilizing that I didn't feel it for about a minute. But after that minute I was in the worst pain of my life! In that moment of grief, heartache, and pain I knew I needed to find a way out, and I had all the confidence in the world to do just that!

On one of the rare occasions where I was allowed to visit my mom's house without my jailer, I was online looking for jobs so I could break free and get my own place for the first time in life at the age of twenty-seven. I came across an article on craigslist of all places looking for leaders in the nonprofit industry. They were willing to train and it was a competitive program. I thought to myself "this is just what I need." So I applied for the first go round.

I didn't get matched with an organization and just as they were about to start the program and shut down further considerations, another organization joined in and recruited me for their open position. I never felt so relieved in my life! I needed this opportunity like I needed air. Literally two days after I was offered the position I was moving out of his place and into my own. I lost the handle to my car door for it after he broke it off, but the freedom I gained from having the courage and confidence to move on was life altering. It's part of the reason I am still here today!

3

The Love

He was a smooth talking Caribbean man from South Jersey, you know the part right next to Cherry Hill. I was standing in the corner of the club while my best friend at the time was dancing to her heart's content. I was always shy in venues like that because I was afraid no one would pick me up and want to dance with me. Well, this night my Caribbean king was there waiting for an unsuspecting victim such as myself.

He walked over, grabbed my hand and moved my hips so they pressed against him. Little did I know I would never spend another day or night apart from him during our entire affair after that dance. He came to live with me and my family one year into our courtship. He would go to church with me every Sunday and spend endless quality time with my family and I. It was right around this time that the beginning of the end was becoming ever so clear.

One day, he went home to Jersey and little did he know he forgot his phone. I went through it and found several numbers from females he had recently been speaking to. The most hilarious part about it is that every woman he had in his phone was labeled as what he associated with them. For example: "Miss good coochie," "Great head," "Money bags," and me, all the way at the bottom of the list, "My wife."

"Is he serious!!!!" That was the only thought that came to mind I was in such disbelief. I called him and cursed him out so bad. I lost all my religion at that moment.

Needless to say after that he crawled back with his tail between his legs begging for another chance. All I wanted was love, so I was inclined to give it to him, plus I never experienced a love like this before, although he was not my first love.

The time had come for my twenty-sixth birthday, and anyone who knows me knows that my birthday is really the only holiday I go all out for in Saresa's world. He wanted to go all out for me so he surprised me with a five-hundred dollar blackberry phone and a weekend getaway to my favorite city, New York! We had a blast eating at the Red Lobster in Times Square, met Ice T and Coco while there, and got lit beyond our limits. I never would have guessed once we got back home that amazing time would turn into my worst nightmare.

As I was one day enjoying my new phone I had received a call on it from a strange New Jersey number. I answered and on the line was a woman with a distinctive west Indian accent.

"Excuse me, do you know Kevin? He's Antiguan!"

"Ummmm, yes I know him. He's been my boyfriend now for the past three years."

"Three years! OMG I have known him for the past two years and been paying his bills. He has been living with me off and on and acting as a stepfather to my son. I cannot believe this!"

"What!?"

"Yes, and the reason I called you is because he had you stored in his phone as his wife! And yet he is living with me. Also I just gave him money to buy his mother a five hundred dollar blackberry phone!"

"No, he actually brought that for me!"

As you can imagine it only got worse from there. He began calling me on the other line to make sure I wasn't believing her "lies." Unlucky for him I trusted my confidence and knew what the truth was and that is what I believed. Still, in the spirit of believing that I needed a love outside of myself beyond all else, I allowed him back into my life with his tail between his legs again.

"One more time," I thought. I would give him one more chance. That chance turned into six more months of dating and actually shopping for engagement rings. We finally decided on one and put half down payment on it. Little did I know the holy spirit had different plans for me.

Oftentimes the spirit would talk to me in my dreams and this night was no different. But this time a warning came that if I stayed with Kevin I would become a bitter, nagging woman that was worked to the bone without one grain of femininity left within her. The warning was so clear I told him that next day I couldn't do this anymore and it was time for him to leave.

Surprisingly, he left without a fight, knowing clear and well his time was up and his facade could no longer be put up. He knew when the spirit gave me a dream, there was no changing my mind and I would follow it through with the strong conviction of the holy spirit.

4

The Mustard Lexus

I saw this beaming light coming from my mother's smile the first day I saw him. Her light was so bright that day that it brought tears to my eyes to witness it. We were looking for the perfect puppy for me and everywhere we went the perfect one wasn't there. We were at the last and final location on Hulen St. and there he was, the perfect Min-Pin black and tan Chihuahua. My mom and I picked him out immediately, and I adopted him on the spot.

Once I got him home he was so shy and stayed that way for most of the six months that I had him. We had gotten close over those six months he began coming out of his shell. He was so attached to me when I took him outside for walks I didn't even have to put a chain around his neck because he would never leave my side. As I am sure you can gather from my previous chapters, I am big on freedom so that meant a lot to me!

I'll never forget the day he left my life. It was just as dramatic as when he entered. It was 2018, the week of my thirty-second birthday. I had just started a new job and got off late. I was exhausted to the max but my puppy needed to use the restroom something terrible because I was so late getting home. Per usual, I walked him down the stairs of my apartment building without a chain when a tan Lexus came wheezing around the corner, startling my puppy to no end. He was so scared that he ran a mile in under a minute. He ran across six lanes of traffic so fast that not one car hit him. I was sitting there in terror, crying, waiting for him to be hit but he wasn't. This tragedy may have been easier for me to accept if I knew what came of him, but to this day, three years later, I still do not know what happened to him. He ran over an embankment once he got through all the lanes of traffic and I haven't seen him since.

Once I lost my puppy, I cried every night for at least a month straight. After that month passed I was ready to start looking for another puppy to take his place. I searched high and low for seven months, more time than I actually had the dog. Then one Saturday morning, just as I was giving up my search feeling utter defeat, my mother called me.

"Saresa, Pet Smart is having an adoption special! I called the one on Hulen where you got Mookie from and they said they have plenty of Chihuahuas looking for good homes. You should check it out."

"Okay, this is my last time looking after this. I am going to give it a rest because this is so painful and reminds me of the loss of Mookie."

Mookie's full name is Moksha, which in the Indian language means to "transcend death." Little did I know his name would be so prophetic. I finally make it to the Pet Smart and I see a black and tan Chihuahua there looking just like Mookie. However, one of the workers there warned me that he had worms so it would be in my best interest to not adopt him. There I was, sad once more!

"Are there any other Chihuahuas?"

"You're in luck. There is one more. His name is Dior. He's really healthy at only ten months old but he was given up for adoption by the owner because he kept running away from the home and they were scared something would happen to him if they did not find him a more secure home."

My first thought was "the last thing I need is another runner!" So I consulted with my mother. If you haven't been able to deduce yet, she is like my living, breathing spirit guide.

"Mom, this dog is a runner just like Mookie! They put him up for adoption because he ran away so much. Plus, I do not think he's that cute. He's not even black. Here's his picture."

"Girl, that dog is going to be cute. All he needs is some love. I think you should get him. He would be a good fit for you."

So I decided to listen to my mom and adopt Dior. I changed his name to Dijor because he was the color of dijon mustard but I didn't want him to be too confused . I took him to church then home that day, and he hasn't left my side in the last two years, never attempting to run away. In fact, there have been times where he could have run or escaped and he instead chose to check on me.

Because I choose to believe in the goodness of me and that all things are working together for my greatest and highest good, I have been blessed with a better companion than I had from the start.

5

The "Friends"

Man, I honestly don't know where to begin on this one because as I am writing this I feel drained physically and mentally from the not for nothing friends I recently released from my life. These were people I knew for years and years but couldn't get out of their own way long enough to see what I needed as a friend, after years of supporting them. As soon as I decided to stop being the supporting actress and become the starring actress in my own movie . . . OHH they couldn't handle it! So I had to move along. Since I could write a whole book on this chapter alone, I'll just tell you one of the many stories here.

There was a friend of mine who I considered a sister. I was a bridesmaid at her wedding, supporting her through her various mistakes and journey on her way to marriage. I saw the writing on the wall of who she would choose to marry even though I knew deep down it was a mistake—predicted the mistake and still stood by her side when it all blew up in her face! After all of that, she had the audacity to treat me like I did not matter in her life and that my contributions were simply for her to use at her disposal and for her own selfish needs. The saddest part about all this? Sis, doesn't even see this is one of the main reasons her marriage failed. Her lack of respect for what the people around her add to her life.

With people who give us this form of treatment, the only way to teach and to learn that you are deserving is to cut them completely out of our lives and cut off the negative energy that doesn't add to your being as a beloved, confident soul.

Confidence truly begins when you learn and know your worth and demand it either with your presence or your absence!

6

The "Money" & The "Thief"

It felt like I only slept for five minutes and I saw as clear as day—someone had gone into my home and ransacked it. They knew I had some lottery winnings and they wanted to rob me of them. Once I saw I had been ransacked and the robber took what they could, it was immediately brought to my attention that the money I really needed was on my person so the thief wasn't able to steal it from me. This short dream was so real that until this day I haven't forgotten it.

As soon as I awoke from my nap, I knew exactly who God was warning me about. I had been mulling around in my head about this person for the past few weeks. The message kept coming to me that this individual had other motives than they were presenting to me.

There was a spiritual women group starting and I just had to be a part of it. I consider myself to be a lifelong spiritual seeker so this was right up my alley. I went and ended up developing a relationship with the lady who was running the group. Our friendship was built over a spiritual internet group and lasted a full six years without ever meeting in person.

At first I was puzzled by the fact we never met in person, but now—how life has allowed everything to play out—I understand I was being protected. I'm not going to get into too many specifics on what ended the relationship other than that dream I received from spirit was the main cause and light bulb moment I needed to see the truth of our one-sided connection.

> *What I will get into are the specific lessons*
> *I learned by experiencing this relationship.*

Lesson 1: Do not be so trusting or giving with your energy. Understand that everyone has a motive in a relationship. Make sure you are clear with yours in every relationship, as well as what the counterpart is.

Lesson 2: Once you recognize your motives and therefore the other party's motives, make sure you believe it and move accordingly. As Maya Angelou used to say, "When someone shows you who they are, believe them the first time."

Lesson 3: Trust the signs, signals, and your intuition. They will never lead you astray. Your greatest ally is God which translates to your Gut. Trust Him and trust It. They are one in the same.

Lesson 4: Let people give to you first if you are the one who is naturally the giver in most relationships. The key to success in life, not just in relationships, is moderation. So learn to switch things up. Don't do everything as you always have, especially when the normal routine seems to always leave you in the cold. Also, it is important to understand you cannot give to anything or anyone without first receiving what it is you are going to give.

Lesson 5: Only give what you won't mind losing. Even if you aren't a natural giver in a relationship, you still have to keep moderation at the forefront of your mind. Give to yourself first, then you can give to others but give freely, without regret of what you are giving.

Lesson 6: Release the disease to please. Put yourself first in all matters. By doing so, you are helping all parties within the relationship since you can only give from a space of what you first were able to receive.

Lesson 7: Finally, know your worth! When you do not know what you are worth, you tend to devalue what you bring to the table and charge little to nothing for it. What you have could be priceless and yet, if you do not know that, you could be scrounging it away for mere pennies or, even worse, for nothing at all.

7

The Gut

According to news24; seventy-eighty percent of your immune tissue is situated is your gut. The same could be mentioned for seventy-eighty percent of your correct answers to life's questions, they too are found in the gut! Just like the health of a person's gut can determine if they are likely to get sick. The same can be said if a person is likely to make a mistake if they do not pay attention to the cues that the gut is sending them in regards to a particular circumstance.

You see, time and time again life has taught me the most valuable lesson, that my gut is God! When I ignore my gut, I ignore God. I ignore what is most connected to the health of my life as a whole.

Six years of being single is enough to cool the largest of egos. Well at least that is what happened to me. Once I moved to Texas, six years ago my romantic life became a stale mate. But let me be clear that is not to say that I wasn't intimate it's only to say I wasn't INNNNtimate in that time. No one really knew except probably my mom but I would cry myself to sleep because I knew I deserved and wanted true connection.

* * *

I just got done having an amazingly wild night in New York City. As I was walking to Penn station I noticed an eyebrow threading shop and knew I needed to stop because my brows were getting thick at the time. As I was walking up there was a slim very attractive man waiting in front of the walk-up.

"Oh, hey you here to get a haircut?"

"Boy no! I'm here to get my brows threaded!"

As I am sure you can tell by the time I walked back downstairs after getting my brows threaded he was still waiting there for me and my number. I obliged because afro-latino men were truly my thing in the past! We ended up dating seriously for three years. Although they were one of the most fun times of my life it was hell at the same time. His toxicity was intoxicating.

Hurricane Sandy was due to touch ground and for the purposes of this story we will call him "Matt", he just hated being alone during times of a storm so he would of course call me to come to him; 2-hours away no less. Me, just always wanting to be in his presence obliged him and went. However the whole time I was on my way there my gut was telling me I should of stayed home.

Fast forward to a day and a half later; after a night of unbridled passion, laughing, joking and various other party favors it's time for me to go home! And "Matt" doesn't waste any time letting me know so. As I am on the road I notice all the public transportation is closed which is unheard of for NYC.

As I get a little further down the road it starts to snow, and I mean snow foreal! I am in Jersey by this point about an hour from his home and an hour from mine, so turning back would of been pointless. I kept going forth and as I did cars were falling off the road right before my eyes by the time I'm thirty minutes from the Delaware Memorial Bridge there were five cars left on the road including mine.

The last car I saw slide from the road was a large truck that I many times saw firemen use. I was in a 2011 Toyota Camry, and I was literally the last car left that did not slide off of the road into a ditch. Yes, I know my angels were the reason I made it home safe that day, but if I would have listened to my gut I wouldn't have had to have such a traumatic experience which has stuck with me until this day!

Needless to say our love story did not last much past this experience but I am nonetheless grateful for the lessons of "Matt". I am now thirty-five years old growing in love with a man who is fulfilling, a leader, masculine, successful, ambitious and all mine romantically. If I was never put in various circumstances that forced me to learn the lesson of who my gut truly is, I do not believe I would of attracted such a love!

8

Saresa's Prayer

Father, most high God. I come to you now, knowing that you have my best interest in mind. Knowing that I can do all things with you. Knowing that you call me a royal priesthood, I am above and not beneath, I am the head and not the tail. This is the birthright given to me by you. I stand in the true power of me, of who you made me to be, oh God. Knowing that all things are working together for my good.

Lord, I know that what is waiting for me is far better than anything I have yet to experience for that I am so grateful. Lord, I call in your grace and your mercy over my life. I pray oh Lord that your light is a lamp upon my feet. That my feet don't go where you haven't gone ahead of me, oh God! I pray that I am blessed with the opportunity to go everywhere you have gone before me that my presence is meant to grace.

May the many doors with my name inscribed on the inside, open effortlessly for me. May the hearts I am meant to prick be drawn to me with ease and synchronicity. May the blessings that are meant to flow to me come without effort just trust. Trust in you and your strength. May I rely completely on you and your goodness for my well being. May I claim my full birthright and break the generational curses that loom over the heads of my loved ones. May I stand in solidarity with everyone and everything that brings peace, joy and contentment into this world.

Lastly Father, I ask that you be filled with joy because of how I choose to be. I pray that you delight in me, oh Lord. And that every reason I am here is fulfilled before I depart. I thank you, I love you and I trust. Amen.

9

The Pandemic

December 2020, was a personal pandemic for me. I was 350lbs, drinking a bottle of wine a night. Smoking a pack of black and milds or a cigarette every single night on repeat. It was the worst winter storm ever! Texas is not somewhere you want to get caught up at in a storm because the state is just not prepared for it.

Everyone around me had no power for days on end and if they did have power they experience rolling blackouts. This for me was terrifying because at my home all I have is me and my small puppy. We were blessed to not have those issues the only thing we faced was internet outage but that we could live through.

During the storm and in the midst of my ill health I was also diagnosed with covid19. This for me was destabilizing. I battled so many demons that winter I will remember it for the rest of my life. After all these circumstances I knew it was time for change so I sought it out with every fiber of my being.

But before I could get there one day I felt chest pains that truly unnerved me, so I went to the ER because I was not sure if it was covid related or not. When I went they ran so many tests and all of them came back healthy the only thing wrong with me was my blood pressure and before this moment I was unaware of any blood pressure issues but this one incident certainly made me aware.

My blood pressure sky rocketed to 234/120 even after they gave my pills to make it stabilize, I literally at stroke level. As I am writing this my body is literally having a reaction at just the memory. As I lay there thinking every miserable thought my mind could muster, per usual the spirit of the Lord came to me. He acknowledged what I was going through but informed me I held the power over this situation and I needed to change the way I was living. I heard his voice tell me I would be discharged by 9pm CST and do you know two hours later at 8:50pm the doctor came in to inform me I was going to be released at 9pm because my blood pressure has dropped down enough. I was so grateful in that moment and haven't looked back since.

But in the spirit of authenticity and transparency I lost about sixty pounds of my excess weight on my own without assistance but the other sixty I was able to secure help through getting a gastric bypass which has truly been beneficial for me losing even more weight. I have not shared with everyone this part of my journey because I do not feel its necessary but I want to tell my authentic story in case someone out there is struggling with the choice. Get the help you need, you will never regret it!

My life just like the world is still healing from it's own personal pandemic but I am grateful to say I am truly enjoying the journey.

10

The Lady Who Harvest

> LET US NOT BECOME WEARY IN DOING GOOD, FOR AT THE PROPER TIME WE WILL REAP A HARVEST IF WE DO NOT GIVE UP.
>
> – GALATIANS 6:9

This is my course in confidence. Each of us is writing our own. I hope these stories of loss and triumph have illustrated for you that the path of confidence is not a straight one. It comes with many complications along the way. I've found through my journey that there are four main components to truly tapping into your confidence.

Component 1: Take the time to truly know yourself. You must do this without any interruptions or outside influence. You have to know who you are in sickness and in health. You have to know what your deepest, darkest fears are. What gets you out of bed in the morning and what keeps you in at night. You have to know your strengths, your weaknesses, and all the parts of you that exist in between. You have to get well acquainted with yourself on all levels to have true confidence.

Component 2: Embrace yourself and all your magical uniqueness. Once you fully know who you are, it is important to welcome you to you! You have to put out all the stops when embracing yourself. I mean the red carpet, the roses, and whatever else it takes to allow yourself to know unequivocally there is none before you and there will be none after you! You have to embrace yourself as if you are courting yourself. When a man courts a woman what does he do? He makes sure that she knows she is the only woman for him. He will go to the ends of the earth to make it known to that one woman. And this is precisely what you must do for yourself.

Component 3: "To thine own self be true." We often recite this quote from Hamlet but we don't live by it. True confidence comes from being true to yourself because you recognize the value you bring to any table. You know anyone should be so lucky to have you seated at the head. You know this because you've taken the time to learn you, embrace you, and now it's time to put into practice what you've done in private. Stand by your principles, morals, opinions, and values because no matter how the tables turn they will never leave you hanging!

Component 4: Name your price, charge tax, shipping, and handling, plus a convenience fee. Being confident is owning it and knowing the price you label yourself with directly reflects the value you place on yourself and your contributions in all situations. Naming your price is all about value. It may not be about money at all. The price could be emotional investment or anything for that matter, but know that confident people come with a higher price because they are confident in what they bring to any table. A person who is less convinced of their talents and contributions wouldn't dare charge what a confident contributor does.

TRUST YOUR PROCESS AT EVERY TURN AND FIRST AND FOREMOST LOOK TO GOD AND YOUR LIFE FOR THE ANSWERS YOU SEEK AS THEY WILL NEVER LEAD YOU ASTRAY. NOW HE WHO SUPPLIES SEED TO THE SOWER AND BREAD FOR FOOD WILL ALSO SUPPLY AND INCREASE YOUR STORE OF SEED AND WILL ENLARGE THE HARVEST OF YOUR RIGHTEOUSNESS.

-2 CORINTHIANS 9:10

Tips & Tricks for the 4 Components

You have to look at your relationship with yourself the same way you look at a relationship with a possible suitor or love interest. The more you invest in the relationship, the greater the return. But what's so great about the self-love relationship is that the risk is much less when betting on yourself versus betting on someone else because you can never predict someone else's behavior. However, you can control your own. So you are investing on a guaranteed return when investing in yourself and your relationship with yourself. When you invest in relationships with others, you are taking a 50/50 risk it could pay off or it couldn't.

Here are a few tips and tricks (aka T&Ts) I've learned over the years when it comes to mastering my self-love journey and the relationship I have with myself.

Component 1

T&T #1: Always focus on what you perceive as right within yourself but don't be afraid to confront what needs healing. So focus on what's right but address what isn't. Balance is key as you discover loving yourself—never abandon it, as it will serve with the next T&T.

T&T #2: Fill your days with focus on your priorities and what matters to your well-being. Take time each day to sip your tea, read that book, eat a healthy meal, and take a soothing bath.

T&T #3: Figure out what makes you tick by starting as a non-active observer of your daily responses. Start to see yourself outside of yourself by looking at what you do in various situations without judgment. You should look to shift paradigms when dealing with the self. Shift from judgment to observation. Once you can truly see yourself objectively, you will be able to self correct and navigate from the highest parts of yourself.

Component 2

T&T #1: Radical acceptance! I mean accept everything about you. Once you know who you are, you have to accept him/her without remorse. We live in a world that teaches us that our natural nature isn't necessarily what we should be, but I am here to tell you that you are exactly how you are meant to be and you should love you and accept you with all the vigor you can muster. Accept your strengths, your weaknesses, and your challenges. Through this radical acceptance you open yourself up to receive all that is naturally yours—your full birthright!

T&T #2: Live out loud! I know this is such a cliche and we have heard this many times over the years, but it is an important concept. Don't just embrace your truths, incorporate them in as many aspects of your life and being as possible. You should be inspired by your life as much as possible and if you are not, you need to sit yourself down and have a talk with you. How can I maneuver differently out here? How can I get inspired by just being? What is the truest expression of me and how can I incorporate him/her in my life?

Component 3

T&T #1: I do not care who it is. If they are expressing to you or exuding energy that you are less than a child of God, the head and not the tail, above and not beneath, then they shouldn't be in your auric field. People who do not see your true worth and the true blessing of having you in their lives don't deserve to have you in them. It's time to choose you and put nothing and no one before you! "And the Lord shall make thee the head, and not the tail; and thou shalt be above only, and thou shalt not be beneath, if thou hearken unto the commandments of the Lord thy God which I command thee this day, to observe and to do them" (Deut. 28:13).

T&T #2: Take back your power and energy. If you do not take care of yourself first, then you cannot take care of anyone else. Stop letting past enemies and "frenemies" live in your mind rent free. If people don't raise your vibration they shouldn't have access to it. I mean they shouldn't have access to it in your thinking *or* your physical reality. All that will do is bring you down and lower your stock. We are on an elevated path not the mediocre path that so many choose to follow.

Component 4

T&T #1: Don't be afraid to be vulnerable and stand in your power. In order to be in your power, you have to be authentic. In order to be authentic, you have to be vulnerable. One cannot exist without the other. Learn to embrace vulnerability. It will lead you to embracing that inner baddie that no one can stop or beat! Standing in your power gives you the proper perspective on just how valuable you are. Once you know that power and value, girl/guy/them/they/you better charge it!

www.ingramcontent.com/pod-product-compliance
Lightning Source LLC
Chambersburg PA
CBHW062207100526
44589CB00014B/1991